# CAPTIVATING COUPLES

# CAPTIVATING COUPLES

David Baird

MQP

# INTRODUCTION

Finding the right actors for a movie is a fine art, and perhaps the greatest challenge for any casting director is getting the formula for a romantic pairing just right. If the chemistry isn't there between the leading couple, then the film is doomed to fail in its quest to charm and captivate audiences. No matter how good the script is, the movie may just fall flat on its face. With the success of a picture hanging on this vital process, and with immense financial risks involved, there can be no mistakes here or a potential hit could become an unmitigated disaster.

The rules for casting romantic leads are not carved in stone—what worked in one film could just as easily ruin another. It is not unheard of for a screen couple to perform memorable love scenes while not being able to stand the sight of each other. At the same time, in another studio, two actors step in front of the camera and find they lose their vital spark the moment the director calls, "Action!" This is the world of moviemaking…things are not always what they seem.

Only recently, the magical aura that has surrounded *Casablanca* for decades was put in a new light by insights from the actors' families into the off-screen relationship of one of cinema's most enchanting couples, Humphrey Bogart and Ingrid Bergman. Heartthrob Tony Curtis has also set the record straight about working with beautiful bombshell Marilyn Monroe on *Some Like It Hot*. No doubt, as time goes by, more secrets will come to the surface about what was really going on beneath the tender looks, smiles, and passionate kisses of some of cinema's most memorable romantic scenes.

As painful as some casting decisions must have seemed at the time, we owe a debt of gratitude to those stars who, for whatever reason, chose not to pick up their option or failed to make the final cut. Not forgetting the daring actors who, despite personal reservations or the odds being stacked against them, trusted the alchemy of the filmmakers to lead them on to create pure screen gold.

Making a movie is a voyage and recruiting a couple to captivate audiences is a stormy business—many are lost at sea along the way. Indeed there is more human debris floating along in the wake of a successful film that one could possibly imagine! Nevertheless, many movies—and couples—manage to brave the tempest and sail on in the warm glow of critical acclaim to become immortalized on the silver screen. This book is a salute to all the intrepid and visionary directors, producers, actors, and financial backers who managed to see beyond the obvious, set sail, and risk all to bring us cinema's most precious cargo—captivating couples.

JOE: Where did you learn to kiss like that?
SUGAR: I used to sell kisses for the milk fund.
JOE: Tomorrow, remind me to send a check for
$100,000 to the milk fund.

### SOME LIKE IT HOT
Tony Curtis & Marilyn Monroe (1959)

FILM FACT: After numerous takes of the famous kissing scene on the yacht, Tony Curtis was alleged to have complained that kissing Marilyn Monroe was "like kissing Hitler." Putting the record straight some years later, Curtis said, "You know, what interrupted us was that quote that I was supposed to have said after that kissing scene with her, which I never did. And someone got back to her with it, and she was offended by it, and I don't blame her. So I called her and we talked for a moment, and she understood that it was never said by me."

Life has taught us that love does not consist in gazing at each other, but in looking outward together in the same direction.

Antoine de Saint-Exupéry

 ## Titanic
Leonardo DiCaprio & Kate Winslet (1997)

FILM FACT: Apparently, when Kate Winslet finished reading the script she wept and knew immediately that she had to have the part. She phoned director Jim Cameron to say he would be mad not to cast her opposite Leonardo DiCaprio whom Winslet felt was a genius. When DiCaprio began to waiver about playing the part of Jack, she took it upon herself to collar him in his hotel at Cannes to tempt him to sign.

In love, there is always one who kisses
and one who offers the cheek.

French proverb

 CARMEN JONES
Harry Belafonte & Dorothy Dandridge (1954)

FILM FACT: The beautiful and talented actress Dorothy Dandridge became the
first African American to receive an Academy Award nomination for Best
Actress in 1954, although Hattie McDaniel won Best Supporting Actress for
*Gone with the Wind* several years earlier. Dandridge also had a fine singing
voice and enjoyed a career as an established singer, as did her co-star in
*Carmen Jones*, Harry Belafonte. However, they both had their singing voices
dubbed for this film by professional opera singers as neither had the training
nor the range to sing operatic roles.

# His strength is so tender,
# his wildness so meek.

James Russell Lowell

 ### CHOCOLAT
### Johnny Depp & Juliette Binoche (2000)

FILM FACT: For two actors so perfectly paired as on-screen lovers in the delicious movie *Chocolat*, their tastes differ enormously. Johnny Depp admitted that quality chocolate is above him and that he prefers the cheaper mass-produced varieties, whereas Juliette Binoche was so focused on her role as a *chocolatier* that she spent time in a Paris chocolate shop learning how to make the real thing.

CAPTAIN VON TRAPP: There isn't going to be any Baroness…. You can't marry someone when you're in love with someone else.

THE SOUND OF MUSIC
Christopher Plummer & Julie Andrews (1965)

FILM FACT: It is rumored that the incredibly romantic scene between Maria (Julie Andrews) and Captain von Trapp (Christopher Plummer) in the gazebo was not originally supposed to be filmed in silhouette. Allegedly, the scene had to be changed because Julie Andrews simply couldn't contain her laughter and kept giggling at the absurd notion of singing so close to someone else's face!

JUDY: All my life, I've been…I've been waiting for someone to love me, and now I love someone. And it's so easy. Why is it so easy now?

### REBEL WITHOUT A CAUSE
James Dean & Natalie Wood (1955)

FILM FACT: Child star Natalie Wood was first considered too wholesome and naive to play the role of Judy, James Dean's love interest, in a film billed as a "challenging drama of today's juvenile violence!" In an attempt to appear more mature to the director and producer, she set about changing her appearance and became a smoker.

# JULIET: You kiss by the book.

 ## ROMEO AND JULIET
Leonardo DiCaprio & Claire Danes (1996)

FILM FACT: Natalie Portman, now best known for the *Star Wars* prequels, was originally considered for the role of Juliet. However, she was only a tiny thirteen year old at the time and when she did screen tests with twenty-one-year-old Leonardo DiCaprio, the age difference apparently made the love scenes look almost obscene. Portman said in an interview that "it looked like Leonardo was molesting me when we kissed" and that she and director Baz Luhrmann both agreed she was too young. Claire Danes eventually took on the role and even Portman agreed that she "did a really really wonderful job."

SLIM: You know how to whistle, don't you, Steve? You just put your lips together and blow.

**To Have and Have Not**
Humphrey Bogart & Lauren Bacall (1944)

FILM FACT: Humphrey Bogart and Lauren Bacall, who was only nineteen years old at the time, fell in love while making *To Have and Have Not*, the young actress's first film. This made director Howard Hawks so jealous that he unkindly said that Bogart had fallen for her character, not Bacall herself, and she would have to keep playing the part for her entire life.

We are in love's land to-day;
  Where shall we go?
Love, shall we start or stay,
  Or sail or row?

Algernon Charles Swinburne

## HIGH SOCIETY
### Bing Crosby & Grace Kelly (1956)

FILM FACT: This wonderful musical version of *The Philadelphia Story* was to be Grace Kelly's last movie before retiring from acting to play her most famous role—that of wife to Prince Rainier of Monaco. As if to make her forthcoming marriage abundantly clear, the large diamond engagement ring she wears throughout the film is the real one given to her by her royal fiancé.

CLEOPATRA: You will kneel.
MARC ANTONY: I will what?
CLEOPATRA: On your knees.

### CLEOPATRA
Richard Burton & Elizabeth Taylor (1963)

FILM FACT: When shooting moved, lock, stock, and barrel to Italy, the already troubled production of *Cleopatra* ran into yet more difficulties. The producers found themselves with a strike on their hands, brought about in response to the over-amorous Italian male extras who found it impossible to resist pinching the bottoms of the female extras playing Cleopatra's servants!

He took the bride about the neck and kissed her lips with such a clamorous smack that at the parting all the church did echo.

William Shakespeare

## THE BRIDE CAME C.O.D.
James Cagney & Bette Davis (1941)

FILM FACT: Bette Davis once said that she and James Cagney had great fun making this classic screwball comedy, but that in her opinion it was a mediocre effort. Audiences obviously disagreed because *The Bride Came C.O.D.* was a big hit in 1941 and to see Davis—the queen of tragedy—bent over Cagney's lap and having cactus spines removed from her backside is a legendary comic moment!

MARISA: I only came to tell you that this, you and me, can't go anywhere beyond this evening. It just can't.
CHRIS: Well, then, you should've worn a different dress.

## Maid in Manhattan
Ralph Fiennes & Jennifer Lopez (2002)

FILM FACT: When asked how much she could identify with her character Marissa, a Latina maid from the Bronx, Jennifer Lopez said that making the film brought back a lot of memories for her. It made her realize how close she was to the character she was playing, as she grew up in the Bronx herself, and filming there put her back into familiar territory.

LAURA: I want to remember every minute, always, always to the end of my days.

 **BRIEF ENCOUNTER**
Trevor Howard & Celia Johnson (1945)

FILM FACT: They are so perfectly matched in this remarkable romantic movie that it is difficult to believe that Trevor Howard was actually eight years younger than Celia Johnson when *Brief Encounter* was made. Howard had suffered an injury while serving with the Royal Artillery in World War II, which lead to him being released early, otherwise he may never have starred in this classic tearjerker at all.

# Love is the only inspiration.

Tagline from the film

 SHAKESPEARE IN LOVE
Joseph Fiennes & Gwyneth Paltrow (1998)

FILM FACT: Joseph Fiennes and Gwyneth Paltrow play the star-crossed lovers in this endearing and excellently-written romantic comedy that the Bard himself would have enjoyed. The versatile Paltrow, in truth an American actress, won a Best Actress Oscar for playing an English Elizabethan character, Lady Viola De Lesseps, who in turn pretends to be a young male actor, Thomas Kent, who in turn plays the tragic young lover Juliet.

CORIE BRATTER: Paul, I think I'm gonna be a lousy wife. But don't be angry with me. I love you very much—and I'm very sexy!

 **BAREFOOT IN THE PARK**
Robert Redford & Jane Fonda (1967)

FILM FACT: Robert Redford and Jane Fonda play newlyweds on a tight budget who rent a sixth-floor apartment at the top of a horrendous flight of stairs—no elevator here! The running gag in the movie is that anyone who visits them arrives breathless and exhausted. However, in the version dubbed for France, where such buildings are commonplace, they had to raise it to the ninth floor so that French audiences could share in the joke.

ROBERTO SANTOS: I took one look
at you and knew I had to kiss you.

 LATIN LOVERS
Ricardo Montalban & Lana Turner (1953)

FILM FACT: Glamorous movie star Lana Turner
began a real life love affair with actor Fernando
Lamas after they met on the set of the highly
successful film *The Merry Widow*, in 1952. The
producers of *Latin Lovers* were keen to recreate
the pair's magic, but the couple broke up just
before filming began and Turner insisted Lamas be
replaced. Fortunately for the filmmakers, Latino
heartthrob Ricardo Montalban, who replaced him,
was more than capable of setting pulses racing.

ROSLYN: How do you find your way back in the dark?
LANGLAND: Just head for that big star straight on.
The highway's under it—it'll take us right home.

## THE MISFITS
Clark Gable & Marilyn Monroe (1961)

FILM FACT: Not only is this a beautiful and poignant drama about the death of the Old West, it is also the last completely finished film ever made by both of its stars. Screen legend Clark Gable was fifty-nine when he died just days after completing *The Misfits*, and movie icon Marilyn Monroe was only thirty-five years old when she tragically died part way through filming her next movie *Something's Got To Give*, just over a year later.

SANDY: I'm going back to Australia.
I might never see you again.
DANNY: Don't talk that way, Sandy.
SANDY: But it's true. I just had the
best summer of my life and now I
have to go. It isn't fair.

## GREASE
John Travolta & Olivia Newton-John (1978)

FILM FACT: To accommodate Australian actress
Olivia Newton-John, who was always the filmmakers
first choice for the role, the original "all-American
girl" Sandy Dumbrowski of the Broadway musical was
changed to Sandy Olsson, a foreign exchange
student from Down Under. The ballad "Hopelessly
Devoted to You" was also written especially for
Newton-John at the last minute, so she would have
her own solo.

# A love caught in the fire of revolution.

Tagline from the film

## DOCTOR ZHIVAGO
Omar Sharif & Julie Christie (1965)

FILM FACT: Rod Steiger, who played villainous politician Victor Komarovsky in this epic love story, caught Julie Christie by surprise more than once with his unusual acting methods during filming. In one scene, where the script calls for her to slap him, he unexpectedly slapped her back. In another, when he was just supposed to kiss the actress, he caught her unawares with a full French kiss that apparently made her squirm.

MR. KHOLI: You know what they say.
No life without wife.

 **BRIDE AND PREJUDICE**
Martin Henderson & Aishwarya Rai (2004)

FILM FACT: This quirky "Bollywood meets Hollywood" adaptation of Jane Austen's *Pride and Prejudice* was model and Indian film star Aishwarya Rai's first movie performed entirely in English. She didn't want her interpretation of the character to be influenced in any way, so she refused to read Austen's classic novel before filming began. Instead she heroically piled on nearly two stone in weight to break away from her fashion model image and add realism to her character.

He was young, handsome, a millionaire—and he'd just pulled off the perfect crime! She was young, beautiful, a super sleuth—sent to investigate it!

Tagline from the film

 ### THE THOMAS CROWN AFFAIR
Steve McQueen & Faye Dunaway (1968)

FILM FACT: This is claimed to have been Steve McQueen's favorite of all the great films he made during his illustrious acting career. When you consider that the minute-long kissing scene between him and screen goddess Faye Dunaway took almost eight hours to film over several days, it really is little wonder why!

Kisses are the language of love, so let's talk it over.

American proverb

## LOVE ME TONIGHT
Maurice Chevalier & Jeanette MacDonald **(1932)**

FILM FACT: Director Rouben Mamoulian used pioneering film techniques in *Love Me Tonight* which were extremely advanced for the 1930s, including the use of zoom lenses and slow motion—breaking moviemaking rules just as they were becoming established. The saucy innuendos in the plot were also a new development, but nothing could hide from his wife the rumor that while Maurice Chevalier was busy making love to Jeanette MacDonald on screen, he was also doing the same off screen with actress Marlene Dietrich.

MAGGIE: Living with somebody you love can be lonelier than living entirely alone—if the one you love doesn't love you.

### CAT ON A HOT TIN ROOF
Paul Newman & Elizabeth Taylor (1958)

FILM FACT: Movie legend Elizabeth Taylor managed to give the performance of a lifetime as Maggie, the passionate, frustrated wife of ex-footballer Brick (Paul Newman) in this adaptation of Tennessee Williams's Pulitzer Prize-winning play. This is even more impressive given the fact that only a week into shooting, her beloved husband Mike Todd was tragically killed in an airplane accident.

SERGEANT WARDEN: I've never been so miserable in my life as I have since I met you.

KAREN HOLMES: Neither have I.

SERGEANT WARDEN: I wouldn't trade a minute of it.

KAREN HOLMES: Neither would I.

 **FROM HERE TO ETERNITY**
Burt Lancaster & Deborah Kerr (1953)

FILM FACT: Deborah Kerr, or "the English virgin" as she was dubbed within her profession, really landed on her feet when Joan Crawford, who had been earmarked for the role of lonely army wife Karen Holmes, dropped out of this production because she didn't like her costumes. This happened just as Deborah Kerr's contract with MGM was coming to an end and the hit movie immediately placed her name right back up there—in bright lights!

She walked off the street, into his life and stole his heart.

Tagline from the film

 **PRETTY WOMAN**
Richard Gere & Julia Roberts (1990)

FILM FACT: There is a magical little moment in this film when Edward (Richard Gere) presents Vivian (Julia Roberts) with an extremely expensive necklace in a jewelry box for their night at the opera. As she reaches out her hand for the necklace, he snaps the lid closed, only narrowly missing her fingers. She jumps and they both laugh in a very natural and touching way. Like so many great screen moments, this was improvised on the spot by Richard Gere and left in the movie for the audience to enjoy.

55

OLIVER BARRETT IV: What can you say about a twenty-five-year-old girl who died? That she was beautiful and brilliant? That she loved Mozart and Bach, the Beatles, and me?

**LOVE STORY**
Ryan O'Neal & Ali MacGraw (1970)

FILM FACT: With the budget severely depleted and not enough money left in the pot to fund the necessary permits to complete filming in New York, the makers of *Love Story* were apparently compelled to adopt stealth tactics. Using only a skeleton crew, they set out to secretly capture the highly effective and moving final scenes of Oliver's solitary walk through snow-covered New York.

LARRY: Maria, do you want to dance with me?… Well then, how about spending the rest of your life with me?

 ## Cousins
### Ted Danson & Isabella Rossellini (1989)

FILM FACT: The French romantic comedy *Cousin, Cousine* caused a sensation in 1975 by gently ridiculing middle-class hypocrisy and presenting sex as really quiet good fun. *Cousins* is a rare achievement—an American remake that, even having lost some of the French film's carnal feistiness, remains as good as the original. Reworked completely for America, it still manages to retain some of its European feel, probably due to a glowing performance by Isabella Rossellini, who here bears more than a fleeting resemblance to her stunning actress mother, Ingrid Bergman.

ILSA: Kiss me. Kiss me as if it were the last time.

## CASABLANCA
Humphrey Bogart & Ingrid Bergman (1942)

FILM FACT: It was widely reported following interviews with the families of Ingrid Bergman and Humphrey Bogart on the sixtieth anniversary release of this classic movie, that the stars didn't really get on during filming. Bergman's actress daughter, Isabella Rossellini, said the couple "weren't even friends." This finally and decisively put an end to decades of rumors about an off-screen love affair between the two stars. But whatever their real relationship, the couple's on-screen chemistry is undeniable and still made for a truly unforgettable and magical movie.

ANNA: How do you explain, your majesty, that many men remain faithful to only one wife?
KING MONGKUT: They are sick.

### THE KING AND I
Yul Brynner & Deborah Kerr (1956)

FILM FACT: "The melting Miss Kerr" is how the actress came to refer to herself having lost twelve pounds in weight after dancing and singing under the hot lights during the shooting of this movie. This was put down to the fact that her gowns, designed by Irene Sharaff, with all their hoops, pleats, and petticoats, weighed between thirty and forty pounds each—about the same weight as the equipment a soldier carries into battle.

# She was lost from the moment she saw him.

Tagline from the film

 **THE FRENCH LIEUTENANT'S WOMAN**
Jeremy Irons & Meryl Streep (1981)

FILM FACT: This complex movie about forbidden love was based on a best-selling novel by John Fowles, but adapted to be a film-within-a-film, with Jeremy Irons and Meryl Streep playing both a pair of Victorian lovers and the modern actors playing those roles in a movie. Several critics were rather unfair about Streep's accent in the film. Given the triple intellectual process involved for an American woman portraying a modern American actress who is, in turn, playing a nineteeth-century English woman, she really did a splendid job.

# Whatever our souls are made of, his and mine are the same.

Emily Brontë

 ## MISSISSIPPI MASALA
### Denzel Washington & Sarita Choudhury (1991)

FILM FACT: Acclaimed-director Mira Nair admits she had difficulty capturing the imagination of the American film studios to get the financial backing she needed to make this impressive and heartfelt cross-cultural love story. The concept of clashing an Indian family from Africa with an African American family all living in the American South proved a hard one to sell. One studio head came straight out and said that the problem was that none of the lead actors were white—to which Nair replied, "Don't worry, all the waiters will be."

My girl she's airy, she's buxom and gay;
Her breath is as sweet as the blossoms in May;
  A touch of her lips it ravishes quite:
She's always good natur'd, good humour'd, and free;
She dances, she glances, she smiles upon me;
  I never am happy when out of her sight.

Robert Burns

### GIRL CRAZY
Mickey Rooney & Judy Garland **(1943)**

FILM FACT: By the time she made this movie, Judy Garland was considered Queen of the MGM film lot. The original director Busby Berkeley, whom she is said to have loathed, only lasted long enough to shoot one number—the finale "I Got Rhythm"—before he was replaced. Garland hated filming the scene because Berkeley had cowboys letting off guns all around her while she was singing, but her close friend and co-star Mickey Rooney managed to persuade her to do it.

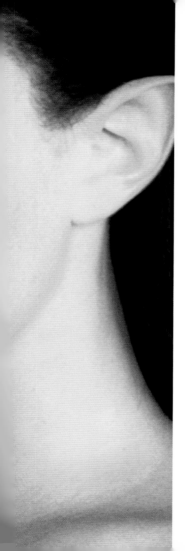

ARWEN: The light of the Evenstar does not wax and wane. It is mine to give to whom I will, like my heart.

### THE LORD OF THE RINGS: THE TWO TOWERS
Viggo Mortensen & Liv Tyler (2002)

FILM FACT: Actor Stuart Townsend was originally chosen to star as Aragorn opposite Liv Tyler's Arwen in the *Lord of the Rings* trilogy, but he had to leave the production early into shooting and was brilliantly replaced by Viggo Mortensen. Despite the cast being urged not to engage in any rough activities, Viggo found the surfing in New Zealand a great temptation and, after one dramatic wipe out, he ended up with a very bruised face which makeup could not cover up. Director Peter Jackson worked around the problem by only filming the star in profile until he healed.

How can a bishop marry? How can he flirt? The most he can say is, "I will see you in the vestry after service."

Sydney Smith

 **THE ANGEL WORE RED**
Dirk Bogarde & Ava Gardner (1960)

FILM FACT: It is hard to believe of such a famous matinee idol, but actor Dirk Bogarde suffered terribly from stage fright and once said, "you can't be as frightened as I am now and still be alive." He managed to overcome his fears when making movies, however, even controversial ones such as this tale of a priest falling in love with a prostitute.

Let me not to the marriage of true minds
Admit impediments. Love is not love
Which alters when it alteration finds,
Or bends with the remover to remove:
O no! it is an ever-fixed mark
That looks on tempests and is never shaken.

William Shakespeare

 ## SENSE AND SENSIBILITY
Hugh Grant & Emma Thompson (1995)

FILM FACT: The charming, talented, and highly intelligent actress Emma Thompson not only starred in this joyous adaptation of Jane Austen's romantic satire, she also wrote the screenplay—and won an Oscar for doing so! If that wasn't enough, Thompson even had the foresight to document the daily business of shooting the movie in her diaries, which have since been published and give a great insight into the whole event.

BRAD ALLEN: Look, I don't know what's bothering you, but don't take your bedroom problems out on me.
JAN MORROW: I have no bedroom problems. There's nothing in my bedroom that bothers me.
BRAD ALLEN: Oh, that's too bad.

**PILLOW TALK**
Rock Hudson & Doris Day (1959)

FILM FACT: The knock-out comedy of the year—literally! Apparently poor Tony Randall, who played Rock Hudson's friend and love rival, Jonathan Forbes, in *Pillow Talk*, suffered the consequences of an overzealous extra when filming the diner scene. Instead of pulling the punch he was to throw at Randall, the extra overshot his mark and actually knocked the actor out! It looked so good on film that the shot still ended up in the final cut.

HARRY: I came here tonight because when you realize you want to spend the rest of your life with somebody, you want the rest of your life to start as soon as possible.

 WHEN HARRY MET SALLY...
Billy Crystal & Meg Ryan (1989)

FILM FACT: Everyone knows the wonderful moment in this movie when Harry and Sally are in a diner discussing orgasms and she decides that the best way to prove her point is to fake one complete with groans, yelps, squeaks, and heavy breathing, right there and then. What many people don't know is that the woman at the next table who so perfectly delivers the hilarious line "I'll have what she's having!" is director Rob Reiner's mother.

MIKE CONNOR: Hello you.
TRACY LORD: Hello.
MIKE CONNOR: You look fine.
TRACY LORD: I feel fine.

## THE PHILADELPHIA STORY
James Stewart & Katharine Hepburn (1940)

FILM FACT: In the days before the voting results became as well-guarded as they are today, word got out that James Stewart was probably not going to attend the Academy Awards ceremony, despite being nominated for his role in this film. Apparently the star received a last minute phone call advising him to put on a dinner jacket and come along. Good job he did— he was awarded Best Actor!

WILLIAM WALLACE: Why do you help me?
PRINCESS ISABELLE: Because of the way
you are looking at me now.

**BRAVEHEART**
Mel Gibson & Sophie Marceau (1995)

FILM FACT: Mel Gibson's beautifully filmed epic *Braveheart* exercised a great deal of artistic license with the historical facts. For instance, the notion that Scottish hero William Wallace had a love affair with Princess Isabelle simply could not be true because the real Isabelle was only a child at that time and was still living in France.

Love guards the roses of thy lips
And flies about them like a bee;
If I approach he forward skips,
And if I kiss he stingeth me.

Thomas Lodge

## THE QUIET MAN
John Wayne & Maureen O'Hara (1952)

FILM FACT: The glamorous and feisty Irish actress Maureen O'Hara managed to break a bone in her hand early on during filming of *The Quiet Man*. It happened while shooting the scene in which John Wayne kisses her for the first time, she tries to slap his face, and he manages to block her blow with his hand. Imagine how hard her slap would have been had it connected with the Duke's cheek!

# Love is not in our choice but in our fate.

John Dryden

 **WEST SIDE STORY**
Richard Beymer & Natalie Wood (1961)

FILM FACT: This classic musical is the story of tragic young lovers Romeo and Juliet relocated to 1950s New York, with the warring families becoming rival gangs—the all-American Jets and their Puerto Rican rivals, the Sharks. Although this is one of the best musicals of all time, the two romantic leads both had their singing dubbed. Jimmy Bryant sang for Richard Beymer, who played Tony, and Marni Nixon sang for Natalie Wood, who played Maria.

MARK WALLACE: If there's
one thing I really despise,
it's an indispensable woman.

## TWO FOR THE ROAD
### Albert Finney & Audrey Hepburn (1967)

FILM FACT: *Two for the Road* ends with a lovely moment, as the newly-reconciled couple head for the French border, which seems to perfectly sum up their marriage. Albert Finney, as Mark, turns to Audrey Hepburn, who plays his wife Joanna, and says, "Bitch!" to which she replies, "Bastard!" and then the two kiss. This language must have seemed quite shocking at the time the film was released and it was probably the closest Hepburn ever came to swearing on screen.

RHETT BUTLER: No, I don't think I will kiss you, although you need kissing, badly. That's what's wrong with you. You should be kissed, and often, and by someone who knows how.

 ### GONE WITH THE WIND
Clark Gable & Vivien Leigh (1939)

FILM FACT: The list of actresses screen tested for the part of legendary Southern Belle Scarlett O'Hara is as long as your arm, and is said to have included Lucille Ball, Mae West, Joan Crawford, Lana Turner, and Katharine Hepburn, to name but a few. This was found to be just part of the publicity hype surrounding the film as it was later alleged that producer David O. Selznick had written a memo back in 1937 saying that British actress Vivien Leigh had already secured the role.

# What a glorious feeling!

Tagline from the film

## SINGIN' IN THE RAIN
### Gene Kelly & Debbie Reynolds (1952)

FILM FACT: Perhaps the best known moment from this timeless musical is the dance routine Gene Kelly performs to the title song "Singin' in the Rain" in a rainstorm which, for the sake of showing up on camera, consisted of water mixed with milk. Less known perhaps is that at the time of filming this incredibly energetic number, the star was fighting a fever and had a temperature that exceeded 103°F!

When a man and a woman have an overwhelming passion
for each other, it seems to me, in spite of such obstacles
dividing them as parents or husband, that they belong to
each other in the name of Nature, and are lovers by
Divine right, in spite of human convention or the laws.

Sebastien-Roch Nicolas De Chamfort

 FRIDA
Alfred Molina & Salma Hayek (2002)

FILM FACT: Charismatic actress Salma Hayek is a lifelong fan of Frida Kahlo's
work and when she heard that director Luis Valdez was considering making a
film about the artist, she asked to play the lead role. Valdez told her she was
too young, and Hayek confidently replied, "Then you are going to have to wait
until I'm old enough." Valdez's film never got off the ground, but Hayek
achieved her dream eight years later when she was given the chance to play
Frida in this film directed by Julie Taymor.

HUBBELL: Katie, it was never uncomplicated.
KATIE: But it was lovely, wasn't it?

### THE WAY WE WERE
Robert Redford & Barbra Streisand (1973)

FILM FACT: One shouldn't forget that not only is Barbra Streisand—who appeared opposite Robert Redford in this landmark film—a superstar actress, she is also a gifted writer, director, and singer. As such, she was invited to sing the unforgettable theme song for this movie which broke as a single in November 1973—and had reached number one by February 1974! It stayed in the charts for over five months and went on to win both an Academy Award and a Grammy.

George had turned at the sound of her arrival. For a moment he contemplated her, as one who had fallen out of heaven. He saw radiant joy in her face, he saw the flowers beat against her dress in blue waves. The bushes above them closed. He stepped quickly forward and kissed her.

E. M. Forster

 A ROOM WITH A VIEW
Julian Sands & Helena Bonham Carter (1986)

FILM FACT: This wonderful adaptation of E. M. Forster's classic novel made stars not only of its impressive young cast, but also of the beautiful Tuscan countryside. The landscape is at its best in the scene when George first kisses Lucy. In the novel, he did so in a field of violets, but as the season dictated there were no violets at the time of filming, a cornfield had to be substituted in the movie.

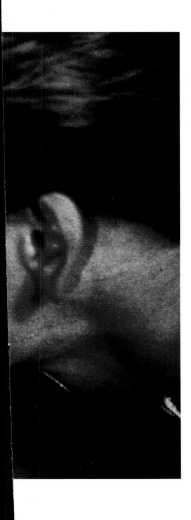

SAM: I love you, Molly.
I always have.
MOLLY: Ditto.

 **GHOST**
Patrick Swayze & Demi Moore (1990)

FILM FACT: Bruce Willis apparently let slip in a late night television interview that he considered playing Sam in this tearjerker, starring opposite his wife of the time Demi Moore. In the end, Patrick Swayze landed the part and the romantic pairing was so effective at tugging audience heartstrings that when the film was screened in Monterrey, Mexico, a cinema is said to have distributed envelopes to the women containing tissues to mop away their tears.

LORD NELSON: I'm only sorry for all the wasted years I've been without you.

## THAT HAMILTON WOMAN
Laurence Olivier & Vivien Leigh (1941)

FILM FACT: Laurence Olivier and Vivien Leigh married in 1940, after divorcing their previous partners, so they began production of *That Hamilton Woman* as newlyweds, brimming over with love, adoration, and romance. Olivier was never shy when it came to expressing his feelings for his beloved wife, "Apart from her looks, which were magical, she possessed beautiful poise.... She also had something else: an attraction of the most perturbing nature I had ever encountered. It may have been the strangely touching spark of dignity in her that enslaved the ardent legion of her admirers."

All women are flirts, but some are restrained by shyness, and others by sense.

François, Duc De La Rouchefoucauld

 ## AN AFFAIR TO REMEMBER
Cary Grant & Deborah Kerr (1957)

FILM FACT: Many people know that this romantic tearjerker proved inspirational to the makers of the 1993 hit *Sleepless in Seattle*, but they don't know that *An Affair To Remember* was itself a remake of a classic 1939 movie called *Love Affair*. Debonair actor and perfectionist Cary Grant and his delightful co-star Deborah Kerr are said to have bounced creative ideas off each other during filming and improvised a great deal of what we see and hear on screen.

Adieu, fair isle! I love thy bowers,
I love thy dark-eyed daughters there;
The cool pomegranate's scarlet flowers
Look brighter in their jetty hair.

Maria Gowen Brooks

 ## MUTINY ON THE BOUNTY
### Marlon Brando and Tarita Teriipia (1962)

FILM FACT: During the filming of *Mutiny on the Bounty*, legendary actor Marlon Brando fell in love with both the delightful islands of Tahiti and his stunning Polynesian co-star Tarita Teriipia, who was then only nineteen years old. The two married in 1962 and later had several children together. Brando went on to buy his own 150-acre Tahitian island called Tetiaroa in 1965.

PAUL VARJAK: I love you.
HOLLY GOLIGHTLY: So what.
PAUL VARJAK: So what? So plenty!

 ### BREAKFAST AT TIFFANY'S
George Peppard & Audrey Hepburn (1961)

FILM FACT: Truman Capote, who wrote the novel *Breakfast at Tiffany's*, wanted Marilyn Monroe to star in the film, and Steve McQueen would probably have been the male lead if he wasn't already under contract for the TV series *Wanted Dead or Alive*, but Audrey Hepburn and George Peppard brilliantly made the characters their own. Despite Hepburn apparently finding method actor Peppard difficult to work with, they made this romantic movie shine and remained close friends until her death.

## Picture credits

All photographs are courtesy of Rex Features picture library.

© 20th Century Fox/Everett Collection/Rex Features: pages 8, 11, 18.
© Columbia Pictures/Everett Collection/Rex Features: page 29.
© New Line Cinema/Everett Collection/Rex Features: page 70.
© Miramax/Everett Collection/Rex Features: pages 45, 94.
Everett Collection/Rex Features: pages 7,12, 30, 32, 35, 41, 46, 49, 54, 57, 66, 74, 77, 78, 85, 99, 105, 109.
Snap Photo Library/Rex Features: pages 3, 15,17, 21, 23, 24, 27, 36, 39, 50, 53, 58, 61, 62, 65, 69, 73, 81, 82, 86, 88, 91, 92, 96, 106.
Rex Features: pages 42, 100, 103.

## Text credits

p.6: Dialogue from *Some Like It Hot* (Ashton Productions/The Mirisch Corporation; screenwriters Billy Wilder and I.A.L. Diamond). p.14: Dialogue from *The Sound of Music* (20th Century Fox/Robert Wise Productions; screenwriter Ernest Lehman). p.16: Dialogue from *Rebel Without A Cause* (Warner Bros; screenwriter Stewart Stern). p.19: Dialogue from *Romeo and Juliet* (20th Century Fox/Bazmark Films; screenwriters Craig Pearce and Baz Luhrman). p.20: Dialogue from *To Have and Have Not* (Warner Bros; screenwriters Jules Furthman and William Faulkner). p.25: Dialogue from *Cleopatra* (20th Century Fox/MCL Films/Walwa Films; screenwriter Sidney Buchman). p.28: Dialogue from *Maid in Manhattan* (Hughes Entertainment/Red Om Films/Revolution Studios/ Shoelace Productions; screenwriter Kevin Wade). p.31: Dialogue from *Brief Encounter* (Cineguild/G.C.F/Rank Organisation Film Productions; screenwriters Noel Coward, Anthony Havelock-Allan, David Lean, and Ronald Neame). p.33: Tagline from *Shakespeare in Love* (Bedford Falls Productions/Miramax Films/Universal Pictures). p.34: Dialogue from *Barefoot in the Park* (Nancy Productions/Paramount Picures; screenwriter Neil Simon). p.37: Dialogue from *Latin Lovers* (Loew's Inc/MGM; screenwriter Isobel Lennart). p.38: Dialogue from *The Misfits* (Seven Arts Productions; screenwriter Arthur Miller). p.40: Dialogue from *Grease* (Paramount Pictures; screenwriter Bronte Woodward). p.43: Tagline from *Doctor Zhivago* (MGM/Sostar). p.44: Dialogue from *Bride and Prejudice* (Bride Productions/Kintop Productions/Pathe Pictures/UK Film Council; screenwriters Paul Mayeda Berges and Gurinder Chadha). p.47: Tagline from *The Thomas Crown Affair* (Simkoe/Solar Productions/The Mirisch

Corporation). p.51: Dialogue from *Cat on a Hot Tin Roof* (Avon Productions/MGM; screenwriters Richard Brooks and James Poe). p.52: Dialogue from *From Here to Eternity* (Columbia Pictures; screenwriter Daniel Taradash). p.55: Tagline from *Pretty Woman* (Silver Screen Partners/Touchstone Pictures). p.56: Dialogue from *Love Story* (Love Story Company/ Paramount Pictures; screenwriter erich Segal). p.59: Dialogue from *Cousins* (Paramount Pictures; screenwriter Stephen Metcalfe). p.60: Dialogue from *Casablanca* (Warner Bros; screenwriters Julius Epstein, Philip Epstein, and Howard Koch). p.63: Dialogue from *The King and I* (20th Century Fox; screenwriters Oscar Hammerstein and Ernest Lehman). p.64: Tagline from *The French Lieutenant's Woman* (Juniper Films). p.71: Dialogue from *Lord of the Rings: The Two Towers* (New Line Cinema/WingNut Films/Lord Dritte Productions/ The Saul Zaentz Company; screenwriters Fran Walsh, Philippa Boyens, and Peter Jackson). p.76: Dialogue from *Pillow Talk* (Arwin Productions/Universal International Pictures; screenwriters Russell Rouse, Maurice Richlin, Stanley Shapiro, and Clarence Greene). p.79: Dialogue from *When Harry Met Sally...* (Castle Rock Entertainment/ Nelson Entertainment; screenwriter Nora Ephron). p.80: Dialogue from *The Philadelphia Story* (MGM; screenwriter Donald Ogden Stewart). p.83: Dialogue from *Braveheart* (20th Century Fox/B.H. Finance/Icon Entertainment/ Paramount Pictures/The Ladd Company; screenwriter Randall Wallace). p.89: Dialogue from *Two for the Road* (20th Century Fox/Stanley Donen Films; screenwriter Frederic Raphael). p.90: Dialogue from *Gone with the Wind* (Selznick International Pictures; screenwriter Sidney Howard). p.92: Tagline from *Singin' in the Rain* (MGM). p.97: Dialogue from *The Way We Were* (Columbia Pictures Corporation/Rastar Productions; screenwriter Arthur Laurents). p.98: Excerpt from *A Room With A View* by E. M. Forster. Used by permission of the Provost and Scholar's of King's College, Cambridge and the Society of Authors as the Literary Representatives of the Estate of E. M. Forster. p.101: Dialogue from Ghost (Paramount Pictures; screenwriter Bruce Joel Ruben). p.103: Dialogue from *That Hamilton Woman* (Alexander Korda Films; screenwriters Walter Reisch and R.C. Sherriff). p.108: Dialogue from *Breakfast at Tiffany's* (Jurow-Shepherd/Paramount Pictures; screenwriter George Axelrod).

We would like to thank the creators both before and behind the camera, who have educated, informed, and entertained us all, especially the many talented screenwriters whose words have enriched this book. To them we are indebted. We apologize for any unintentional error or omission in the acknowledgments above and would be pleased to hear from any companies or individuals who may have been accidentally overlooked.

Published by MQ Publications Limited

12 The Ivories, 6–8 Northampton Street, London, N1 2HY

Tel: +44 (0)20 7359 2244 / Fax: +44 (0)20 7359 1616

Email: mail@mqpublications.com

Website: www.mqpublications.com

ISBN: 1-84072-971-6

1 3 5 7 9 0 8 6 4 2

Printed and bound in Singapore